PLANT DEFENSES

PLANTS THAT POISON

DWAYNE HICKS

PowerKiDS press

New York

Published in 2017 by The Rosen Publishing Group, Inc.
29 East 21st Street, New York, NY 10010

First Edition

Editor: Sarah Machajewski
Book Design: Reann Nye

Photo Credits: Cover Diane Diederich/E+/Getty Images; p. 4 ronstik/ Shutterstock.com; p. 5 Arve Bettum/Shutterstock.com; p. 6 Flegere/Shutterstock.com; p. 7 Bildagentur Zoonar GmbH/Shutterstock.com; p. 8 Jeka/Shutterstock.com; p. 9 Alistair Berg/DigitalVision/Getty Images; p. 10 StevenRussellSmithPhotos/ Shutterstock.com; p. 11 Kenneth Sponsler/Shutterstock.com; p. 12 wasanajai/ Shutterstock.com; p. 13 Caner Cakir/Shutterstock.com; p. 14 Dimijana/ Shutterstock.com; p. 15 Olaf Speier/Shutterstock.com; p. 16 Chris Hill/ Shutterstock.com; p. 17 Starover Sibiriak/Shutterstock.com; p. 18 FineShine/ Shutterstock.com; p. 19 merlinpf/E+/Getty Images; p. 20 picturepartners/ Shutterstock.com; p. 21 photolike/Shutterstock.com; p. 22 Flashon Studio/ Shutterstock.com.

Cataloging-in-Publication Data

Names: Hicks, Dwayne.
Title: Plants that poison / Dwayne Hicks.
Description: New York : PowerKids Press, 2017. | Series: Plant defenses | Includes index.
Identifiers: ISBN 9781499421552 (pbk.) | ISBN 9781499421576 (library bound) | ISBN 9781499421569 (6 pack)
Subjects: LCSH: Poisonous plants–Juvenile literature.
Classification: LCC QK100.A1 H53 2017 | DDC 581.6'59–d23

Manufactured in the United States of America

CPSIA Compliance Information: Batch #BS16PK: For Further Information contact Rosen Publishing, New York, New York at 1-800-237-9932

CONTENTS

SOMETHING BAD

Coughing. Dizziness. Throwing up. Bad headaches. These are **symptoms** of sickness. They can also be a sign that you've eaten something harmful. Could that thing be a plant?

Plenty of plants are edible, which means they can be eaten. Fruits and vegetables are common examples. However, there are also a lot of poisonous plants in the world. Eating—and sometimes just touching—them can make you really sick. The poison from some plants can even kill you.

Plants poison their predators in order to **protect** themselves. It's an amazing defense! Let's learn more about it.

Mushrooms aren't plants—they're **fungi**. They can be as deadly as poisonous plants.

SPECIES SURVIVAL

The natural world has plenty of dangers that **threaten** a plant's survival. Animals, bugs, and other plants can greatly harm or kill plants. Bad weather and poor soil are other examples of challenges plants face. Plants can't get up and move to avoid these dangers. Instead, they've had to **adapt**.

An adaptation is a change that helps a plant survive in its environment. Making poison is an adaptation. Long ago, poisonous plants survived longer than nonpoisonous plants. They lived to pass down this adaptation. Over time, it became part of the **species**.

PLANT POINTER
When talking about plants, "poisonous" means they're able to cause sickness or death if taken into the body.

Some plant poisons will hurt mammals but not birds. The birds can eat the berries and then spread the plant's seeds, helping the plant species survive.

POISON AS DEFENSE

Poison is an adaptation, and it's also a cool plant defense. A defense is a way something protects itself. A plant's poison can greatly harm animals that eat or even touch it. Over time, predators have learned to stay away from poisonous plants. Sometimes predators learn this lesson the hard way. These unlucky ones can get very sick or even die.

Some plant defenses are easy to see, such as thorns, looking sick, or shrinking when touched. However, poison is a chemical defense. Poison is a chemical made inside the plant, so you can't tell if a plant is poisonous just by looking at it.

PLANT POINTER

A chemical defense is when a plant uses chemicals to keep from being eaten. Bad smells are another kind of chemical defense.

Never touch or eat a plant you're unfamiliar with. When you go into nature, take a plant guide with you. It will tell you which plants are safe—and which aren't.

TOXIC OILS

Poison ivy grows in many **habitats**—from the woods to your backyard. Poison ivy has groups of three leaves that sometimes have saw-toothed edges.

It's easy to accidentally brush against or walk through poison ivy. When the plant is touched, it releases a **toxic** oil called urushiol. The oil causes an itchy, painful rash to appear on your skin. Sometimes, the reaction is so bad people have to go to the hospital. After one **encounter** with poison ivy, people know to avoid touching it, and the plant can grow without being bothered.

PLANT POINTER
The poison ivy plant releases urushiol from its leaves, flowers, fruit, stem, and roots. There's no safe way to handle this plant—the oil can even stick to your clothes!

Poison ivy blends in well with
other plants. It's important to
learn how to identify it.

POISONOUS BEADS

The jequirity plant is native to India, but it grows well in warm, tropical habitats around the world. The black-and-red seeds of this plant are used as beads in jewelry and to make instruments. This is surprising because the seeds contain one of the deadliest plant poisons in the world.

Jequirity seeds contain abrin, which is a toxin that's **fatal** if swallowed. People who've **ingested** this toxin will throw up, and their heart and liver may fail. They may die after several days. People who use the seeds to make jewelry can be accidentally poisoned if they prick their finger.

PLANT POINTER
Jequirity seeds have a hard outer coating that keeps the poison safely inside. If people swallow the seeds whole, they might not get sick.

Jequirity plants are sometimes called crab's eyes or rosary peas.

CASTOR-OIL PLANTS

Ricin is an extremely deadly plant toxin. The castor-oil plant contains fatal amounts of ricin in its seeds and smaller amounts in other parts of the plant. Poisoning happens when an animal eats or chews on broken seeds. The poison is released, and the animal that ate the seeds becomes very sick. After a few days, the animal can even die.

Even though castor beans are extremely poisonous, people have been using medicine made from castor oil for thousands of years. Once the oil is removed from the seeds, it's safe to take as medicine in small doses.

PLANT POINTER

Some people grow castor-oil plants in their garden! These plants can grow up to 15 feet (4.6 m) tall.

CASTOR BEANS

Scientists think the castor-oil plant's poison is meant to keep predatory bugs away. One study showed that aphids, which are bugs that suck juice from plants, died within 24 hours of feeding on the plant.

DANGEROUS WEEDS

Around 399 BC, the Greek philosopher Socrates died from drinking the juices of a very deadly plant—poison hemlock. This plant is a weed that grows along the edges of roads, fields, streams, and hiking trails. It grows to be between 3 and 10 feet (0.9 and 3 m) tall and has groups of tiny white flowers.

All parts of the poison hemlock plant are poisonous. It can kill animals and people who eat it. The poison contains a chemical that can shut down an animal's nervous system. This system carries messages from the brain to the rest of the body. That threat is enough to keep predators away!

PLANT POINTER
The poison inside the poison hemlock's seeds is coniine.

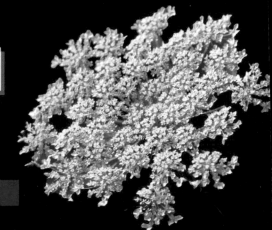

QUEEN ANNE'S LACE

Poison hemlock can be mistaken for Queen Anne's lace. They look alike. Looking like a poisonous plant is another kind of defense—it allows the Queen Anne's lace to stay safe from predators, too.

BEAUTIFUL BELLADONNA

At first glance, the dark, bell-shaped flowers and shiny black berries of the belladonna plant seem very beautiful. To the unlucky people who have tasted the plant, the belladonna is something much worse. It's deadly.

Belladonna is also called deadly nightshade. It's part of a group of plants called the nightshade family. Belladonna's leaves and berries are very poisonous, but the roots are the deadliest part. People who've been poisoned have trouble swallowing and talking. Their eyesight blurs, and they **hallucinate**. They become confused and upset. Poison from the deadly nightshade can kill a person within a few days.

> **PLANT POINTER**
> Eggplants, potatoes, and tomatoes are also in the nightshade family, but they're safe to eat.

EGGPLANT

"Belladonna" means "beautiful lady" in Italian. Long ago, women put drops made from the belladonna plant in their eyes. This made their eyes appear bigger, which people thought was beautiful. Today, we know this is very unsafe!

THE DEVIL'S TRUMPET

Daturas have many types, including jimsonweed, moonflowers, devil's trumpet, and thornapple. Whatever you call these plants, they're poisonous.

Daturas are often seen as weeds in fields and alomg roadsides. They have large, long flowers that are shaped like trumpets. Their fruit has a hard outer coating that's covered with thorns. Every part of these plants is poisonous. When eaten, they make people hallucinate and feel sick, and they can kill them.

Some American Indian cultures have safely used jimsonweed in **rituals**. However, it's not safe for people to do this on their own.

Daturas have other defenses besides poison. They also taste and smell bad, which keeps animals from eating too much of them.

BE CAREFUL!

Plenty of plants produce poison as a way to ward off predators. Poison oak, poison sumac, lily of the valley, wolfsbane, foxglove, and elderberry are also commonly known poisonous plants. Even plants that may seem safe, such as rhubarb and nutmeg, can have toxic effects. No matter what it is, each poisonous plant has the same goal—to survive. If poison can keep predators away, plants will produce it.

It's important to be careful when handling unfamiliar plants. You never know what's going on inside the plant. Is it producing poison? You don't want to make the mistake of finding out!

GLOSSARY

adapt: To change to meet new conditions.

encounter: A meeting with someone or something.

fatal: Causing death.

fungus: A living thing that is somewhat like a plant but doesn't make its own food or have leaves or a green color. Fungi include mold and mushrooms.

habitat: The natural home of an animal or plant.

hallucinate: To see something that is not actually there.

ingest: To take into the body.

protect: To keep safe.

ritual: A ceremony.

species: A group of living things that have similar traits.

symptom: A sign of sickness.

threaten: To cause something to be at risk.

toxic: Poisonous.

INDEX

WEBSITES

Due to the changing nature of Internet links, PowerKids Press has developed an online list of websites related to the subject of this book. This site is updated regularly. Please use this link to access the list: www.powerkidslinks.com/plantd/pois